Pirates in the Media

by John Hamilton

Visit us at
www.abdopublishing.com

Published by ABDO Publishing Company, 4940 Viking Drive, Suite 622, Edina, Minnesota 55435.
Copyright ©2007 by Abdo Consulting Group, Inc. International copyrights reserved in all countries.
No part of this book may be reproduced in any form without written permission from the publisher.
ABDO & Daughters™ is a trademark and logo of ABDO Publishing Company.

Printed in the United States.

Editor: Sue Hamilton
Graphic Design: John Hamilton
Cover Design: Neil Klinepier
Cover Illustration: *Pirates of the Caribbean*, courtesy Walt Disney Pictures; *Pegleg*, ©1996 Don Maitz
Interior Photos and Illustrations: p 1 *Pirates of the Caribbean* cast, courtesy Walt Disney Pictures;
p 3 *Dead Men Tell No Tales*, ©2003 Don Maitz; p 5 front cover of *Treasure Island*, Mariners' Museum;
p 6 Long John Silver, Mary Evans; p 7 Robert Louis Stevenson, Corbis; p 9 cover of *Treasure Island*,
courtesy Turner Home Entertainment; p 10 Ian McKellen as Captain Hook, Corbis; p 11 (top)
Captain Hook fights Peter Pan, Mary Evans; (bottom) Jason Isaacs as Captain Hook, courtesy
Universal Pictures; p 12 *Pirates of Penzance*, Corbis; p 13 *The Black Pirate*, Corbis; p 14 *Captain Blood*,
courtesy Warner Brothers; p 15 *The Sea Hawk*, courtesy Warner Brothers; p 16 *Pirates of the Caribbean*
Disneyland ride, AP/Wideworld; p 17 Johnny Depp & Orlando Bloom, courtesy Walt Disney
Pictures; p 18 Gore Verbinski, Jerry Bruckheimer, Johnny Depp, courtesy Walt Disney Pictures;
p 20 (top) Johnny Depp, courtesy Walt Disney Pictures; (bottom) *Pirates of the Caribbean* cast,
courtesy Walt Disney Pictures; p 21 (top) Jack Sparrow fleeing cannibals; (middle) Norrington,
Turner, Sparrow sword fight; (bottom) Sparrow among the cannibals, all courtesy Walt Disney
Pictures; p 22 scene from *Pirates of the Caribbean: At World's End*, courtesy Walt Disney Pictures;
p 23 poster for *Pirates of the Caribbean: Dead Man's Chest*, courtesy Walt Disney Pictures; p 24 cover
of *The Secret of Monkey Island*, courtesy LucasArts; p 25 screenshot from *Sid Meier's Pirates!*, courtesy
Firaxis Games; pp 26-27 screenshots from *Pirates of the Burning Sea*, courtesy Flying Lab Software;
p 28 (top) *Which Shall be Captain*, Howard Pyle; (bottom) illustration from *Treasure Island*, N.C.
Wyeth; p 29 (top) *Blackbeard's Revenge*, ©2003 Don Maitz; (bottom) *Don the Pirate*, ©2004 Don
Maitz; p 31 *Infamous Jolly John*, ©2006 Don Maitz.

Library of Congress Cataloging-in-Publication Data

Hamilton, John, 1959-
   Pirates in the media / John Hamilton.
      p. cm.
   Includes index.
   ISBN-13: 978-1-59928-764-5
   ISBN-10: 1-59928-764-1
   1. Pirates in mass media. I. Title.

P94.5.P57H36 2007
302.2308--dc22

                                    2006032016

Contents

Treasure Island

Everything we think we know about pirates comes from a handful of sources. One of the most influential is *Treasure Island*, by Scottish author Robert Louis Stevenson (1850-1894). This classic sea tale was first published as a book in 1883, to huge popular acclaim. It is one of the world's best-loved adventure stories. To this day, when people think of pirates, visions from the book pop into their minds: mounds of buried treasure, eye patches, black schooners, and peg-legged buccaneers with parrots perched on their shoulders. Some of these icons have an element of truth, but many are pure fiction. For example, "X marks the spot" on a treasure map sprang entirely from the imagination of Stevenson.

Jim Hawkins, *Treasure Island's* teenage hero, narrates the story. Jim is the son of an innkeeper in 18th-century Bristol, England. Billy Bones, an old buccaneer, is a guest at the inn. He is in possession of a secret treasure map. A group of pirates, including the murderous Blind Pew, ransack the inn, but the brave Jim has already fled with the precious map. He gives it to family acquaintances, Squire Trelawney and Dr. Livesey, who recognize the map as the key to booty left by the notorious pirate Captain Flint. Trelawney hires a ship, the *Hispaniola*, and invites Jim to set sail in search of Treasure Island.

Facing page: The front cover of the 1911 edition of Robert Louis Stevenson's *Treasure Island*, illustrated by N.C. Wyeth.

TREASURE ISLAND

BY

ROBERT LOUIS STEVENSON

"HE WAS BRAVE AND NO MISTAKE"

Above: An illustration of Long John Silver.

Unfortunately, the crew members of the *Hispaniola* are actually pirates, including Long John Silver, the one-legged cook. Once the ship nears Treasure Island, Silver emerges as the leader of the cutthroats. The pirates try to mutiny, but Jim foils their plan. A series of adventures follow. Jim finds himself on the island, with the pirates hot on his trail. He meets old Ben Gunn, a former pirate who had been marooned many years earlier, and who now holds the key to the lost treasure. Long John Silver turns out to be an ally… or is he? Jim is resourceful and brave as he races to find the golden hoard before the pirates, and struggles to get off Treasure Island alive.

Robert Louis Stevenson was born in Edinburgh, Scotland, in 1850, the son of a Scottish lighthouse engineer. His grandfather and great-grandfather also were distinguished lighthouse designers. From this family background, Stevenson inherited his love of the sea, and his spirit of adventure. When his father took the young Stevenson on lighthouse-inspection tours, the boy's head was filled with stories about the islands and hidden inlets of the Scottish coast. When Robert grew into a young man, he knew that he wanted a career in literature. His stern father, however, insisted that his son receive a practical education, so Stevenson studied law. But his first love was writing. He continued selling his stories, with moderate success.

In 1881, when Stevenson was 30 years old, he spent the late summer in a cottage nestled in the mountains of northern Scotland. Stevenson suffered from a lung disease, possibly tuberculosis, and often traveled to mountainous areas to escape the coughing fits that plagued him. Four family members traveled with him that summer, including his parents, his American wife, Fanny, and his stepson, Lloyd Osbourne, who was 12 years old.

Above: Robert Louis Stevenson, author of *Treasure Island*.

Above: The hand-drawn map from Stevenson's 1883 edition of *Treasure Island.*

The weather in the Scottish Highlands was cold and rainy. To pass the time, young Lloyd painted watercolor pictures. One afternoon his stepfather decided to join the fun. As Lloyd later wrote about that fateful day, "… I happened to be tinting a map of an island I had drawn. Stevenson came in as I was finishing it, and with his affectionate interest in everything I was doing, leaned over my shoulder, and was soon elaborating the map and naming it. I shall never forget the thrill of Skeleton Island, Spyglass Hill, nor the heart-stirring climax of the three red crosses! And the greater climax still when he wrote down the words "Treasure Island" at the top right-hand corner! And he seemed to know so much about it too— the pirates, the buried treasure, the man who had been marooned on the island."

The map filled Stevenson with inspiration. Within three days he wrote the first three chapters of his new book, *The Sea Cook, or Treasure Island.* He finished the novel a few months later while on another retreat, this time in Switzerland. It was a roaring adventure story, filled with unforgettable characters and hair-raising action. After finishing the last chapter, Stevenson said, "If this don't fetch the kids, why, they have gone rotten since my day."

The book was first published in installments in *Young Folks* magazine, where it was largely ignored, much to Stevenson's disappointment. But in 1883, the novel was sold as a stand-alone book, this time simply titled *Treasure Island.* The public went wild. *Treasure Island* was Robert Louis Stevenson's first big success as a writer.

Critics and fellow writers heaped praise on the novel. Even though it was written as a children's story, many adults were swept up in the sea tale. England's Prime Minister Ewart Gladstone even stayed up one night until 2:00 A.M. to finish the story. In *Under the Black Flag*, author and naval scholar David Cordingly wrote, "The effect of *Treasure Island* on our perception of pirates cannot be overestimated."

Besides being a stirring adventure story (a "ripping yarn" in Great Britain), *Treasure Island* is filled with nautical terms and the authentic language of sailors. Stevenson knew the sea. He was familiar with many nautical legends and customs. For example, it is no accident that one-legged Long John Silver was the *Hispaniola's* cook. In real life, many ships' cooks were former sailors who had been wounded in battle. A job in the kitchen was the only place left for these men to continue a life at sea.

Robert Louis Stevenson went on to a very successful literary career, penning such classics as *The Strange Case of Dr. Jekyll and Mr. Hyde*, and *Kidnapped*. But it is *Treasure Island* that is his most fondly remembered work.

Several movie versions of *Treasure Island* have been produced over the years, including a very famous 1950 Disney version, which was the company's first complete live-action film.

The character of Long John Silver is colorful and complex. The pirate has been played by such giants of the silver screen as Wallace Beery, Robert Newton, Orson Welles, and Jack Palance. A 1990 made-for-television version of *Treasure Island* starred Christian Bale (*Batman Returns*, *The Prestige*) as Jim Hawkins, and Charlton Heston (*The Ten Commandments*, *Ben-Hur*) as Long John Silver. Heston's son Fraser directed the film. Action packed and true to the novel, many consider it the best live-action version of *Treasure Island* ever made.

Above: Many people consider the 1990 made-for-television version of *Treasure Island* to be the best ever made.

Captain Hook

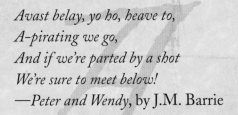

Avast belay, yo ho, heave to,
A-pirating we go,
And if we're parted by a shot
We're sure to meet below!
—*Peter and Wendy*, by J.M. Barrie

Besides *Treasure Island's* Long John Silver, the most famous pirate character in fiction is undoubtedly Captain Hook from J.M. Barrie's beloved *Peter Pan*. The story is about a boy, Peter Pan, who refuses to grow up, spending most of his time on an enchanted island called Neverland. His archenemy is Captain Hook, the pirate whose only purpose in life is to destroy Peter. He hates Peter because during a sword fight the boy cut off the captain's right hand, which has since been replaced by a gleaming hook. A giant crocodile ate the hand, and liked the taste of it so much that the beast has followed the pirate ever since, hoping for more.

Barrie (1860-1937) was a celebrated Scottish novelist and playwright when he published *The Little White Bird*, the 1902 book in which the character Peter Pan first appeared. Two years later, *Peter Pan, or The Boy Who Wouldn't Grow Up* made its London stage debut on December 27, 1904. The play was so popular that in 1911 Barrie adapted it into a novel called *Peter and Wendy*, known today simply as *Peter Pan*.

Top right: Ian McKellen as Captain Hook in the Royal National Theatre's 1997 stage production of *Peter Pan*.

When we speak of pirates, many of the images that spring to mind come directly from Captain Hook. In addition to the iron claw that replaced his hand, the villainous buccaneer is dashing and sinister at the same time. He is an aristocrat who dresses in fine clothes, imitating England's King Charles II, whom Hook is said to resemble. He is intelligent, yet prone to fits of wild emotion. As Barrie described Hook in *Peter and Wendy*, "In person he was cadaverous and blackavized, and his hair was dressed in long curls, which at a little distance looked like black candles… . His eyes were of the blue of the forget-me-not, and of a profound melancholy, save when he was plunging his hook into you, at which time two red spots appeared in them and lit them up horribly."

Over the years, many stage plays and movies have been based on Barrie's story. The most famous is likely the 1953 Disney animated version, *Peter Pan*. The colorful role of Captain Hook has been called a gift to actors. Dustin Hoffman (*Finding Neverland, Rain Man*) played him in Steven Spielberg's 1991 film *Hook*. In P. J. Hogan's 2003 film *Peter Pan*, Jason Isaacs (Lucius Malfoy in the Harry Potter films) played the flamboyant pirate with menacing style.

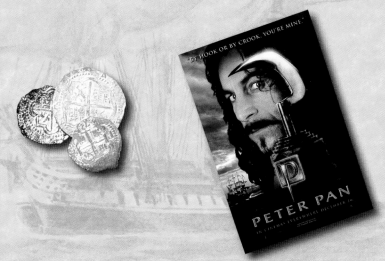

Above: Peter Pan fights Captain Hook in this illustration by Alice B. Woodward in *The Peter Pan Picture Book*, published in 1907. *Left:* Jason Isaacs as Captain Hook in the 2003 feature film *Peter Pan*.

Pirate Drama

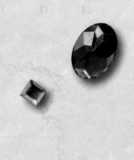

When it comes to drama, pirates are a popular subject. Conflict and action are practically built in: swashbuckling adventure, ship battles, buried treasure, unforgettable characters battling with their cutlasses and wits. It's only natural that for many years pirates have been the subject of stage and screen. Playwrights Gilbert and Sullivan staged their comic opera *The Pirates of Penzance* in 1879, delighting audiences with a funny tale of mistaken identities, pirate kings, and fair ladies. But it was the invention of motion pictures in the first part of the 20th century that brought pirate adventure to the masses.

Above: A stage performance of *The Pirates of Penzance.*

The Black Pirate was one of the first pirate movies. The 1926 silent production starred Douglas Fairbanks, Sr., who dazzled audiences with swordplay and amazing stunts. In the film, Fairbanks plays the Duke of Arnoldo, who becomes the Black Pirate to avenge his father's death at the hands of bloodthirsty buccaneers. He kills a pirate captain in a duel, and then single-handedly captures a Spanish galleon. In an often-imitated signature stunt, the Black Pirate descends from the ship's mast by digging his knife into the canvas and then sliding down to the deck. After taking over the ship, he falls in love with a princess. She is captured by a group of cutthroats, but the Black Pirate and his comrades come to her rescue.

Above: Douglas Fairbanks, Sr., in *The Black Pirate*.

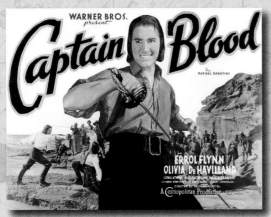

Above: Errol Flynn as Captain Peter Blood.

The Black Pirate was so successful that a flood of other pirate movies soon followed. *Captain Blood*, originally a book written by Rafael Sabatini in 1922, had been turned into a silent film in 1924. In 1935, Warner Brothers created a sound version starring unknown actor Errol Flynn as Captain Peter Blood. In the story, Blood is wrongly convicted of treason against the king, and then sold into slavery on a plantation near Port Royal, on the Caribbean island of Jamaica. He and his fellow slaves eventually escape. After stealing a Spanish ship, they begin new lives as pirates. With its many exciting sword fights and thrilling sea battles, the film was a smash hit, catapulting Flynn into stardom along with his co-star, Olivia de Havilland. The film was nominated for an Academy Award.

Errol Flynn continued his piratical success with Warner Brothers' 1940 film *The Sea Hawk*. Flynn played Captain Geoffrey Thorpe, a dashing privateer who defends England against a treacherous Spanish invasion. The production was very expensive. Two full-sized galleons were constructed for the movie. They were floated in huge tanks on the studio lot, and rocked back and forth using hydraulic jacks. The lavish production and Flynn's increasing popularity helped make the film was a big hit.

As the years passed, even more pirate stories were filmed, until it seemed the movie-going public had finally lost interest. Even occasional big-budget revivals like 1976's *Swashbuckler*, starring Robert Shaw and James Earl Jones, or 1995's *Cutthroat Island*, with Geena Davis, couldn't seem to bring the pirate genre back to its glory days. Then, in 2003, an unlikely pirate hero thrilled moviegoers around the world.

Above: Errol Flynn in *The Sea Hawk*.

Pirates of the Caribbean

On March 18, 1967, the Disneyland theme park in Anaheim, California, unveiled a ride that quickly became an audience favorite: *Pirates of the Caribbean*. Visitors took a 15-minute boat ride through several environments filled with animatronic pirate characters. In one section of the ride, the pirates plunder a Caribbean port, although the musical theme (*Yo Ho, A Pirate's Life for Me*) kept the mood lighthearted.

Pirates of the Caribbean was one of the last rides personally supervised by founder Walt Disney. It was said to be his favorite ride, even though he died shortly before the opening. The ride became so popular that it can now be found in three other Disney theme parks, including Florida's Magic Kingdom, Tokyo Disneyland, and Disneyland Paris.

Right: A scene from Disneyland's *Pirates of the Caribbean* ride.

In 2002, rumors began swirling of a planned movie based on the theme-park ride. Some people were suspicious that the movie would be nothing more than a promotional stunt for the Disneyland ride. Many others were skeptical about the seriousness of the effort. After all, nobody in Hollywood had made a successful pirate movie in decades. *Pirates of the Caribbean*, they warned, was sure to be a colossal failure.

On July 9, 2003, Walt Disney Pictures, together with Jerry Bruckheimer Films, released *Pirates of the Caribbean: The Curse of the Black Pearl*. The story centers on an eccentric yet daring and clever pirate, Captain Jack Sparrow, who seeks a hoard of hidden treasure. He is also on a quest to regain control of his old ship, the *Black Pearl*, which has been taken over by the mutinous Captain Barbossa and his crew of cursed pirates. The evil buccaneers sack Port Royal, Jamaica, and kidnap the governor's daughter, Elizabeth Swann. They believe that she holds the key to lifting their curse of living forever as the undead. The dashing Will Turner, who loves Elizabeth, joins forces with Captain Jack to save her.

Above: Johnny Depp and Orlando Bloom in *Pirates of the Caribbean: The Curse of the Black Pearl.*

The film surprised many people with its riveting action, special effects, and storytelling. Most surprising of all was the performance by Johnny Depp (*Finding Neverland, Charlie and the Chocolate Factory*), who played the movie's lead character, Captain Jack Sparrow. Depp tackled the role with an offbeat gusto, creatively mixing comic timing, slurred speech, and glam-rock eye shadow. Depp has said that in playing Jack Sparrow, he imagined a combination of the cartoon character Pepé Le Pew and the Rolling Stones' Keith Richards. When asked how he created Captain Jack's erratic way of moving, Depp confessed to *Entertainment Weekly* that he resorted to a creative, and probably ill-advised, experiment. Said Depp, "I imagined those pirates out in the open sea in extreme heat, no escape from the sun and humidity, so I thought it would be interesting to jack up the sauna pretty good and see how long I could take it. I cranked it up to, like, 240 degrees. I was cooking. That degree of heat makes you sort of move involuntarily. That's where all of Captain Jack's jerky movements came from."

Johnny Depp received a lot of attention from the press for his role as Jack Sparrow, but other actors had meaty roles in the film as well. Geoffrey Rush (*Mystery Men*, *Shakespeare in Love*) played the clever villain Barbossa, leader of the cursed pirates. Orlando Bloom (*The Lord of the Rings*, *Kingdom of Heaven*) played Will Turner. Elizabeth was played by Keira Knightley (*Bend It Like Beckham*, *Pride & Prejudice*). She was just 17 when she made the film, but gained many admirers for her gutsy performance.

Pirates of the Caribbean: The Curse of the Black Pearl shattered all expectations. Under the rousing direction of Gore Verbinski, it became one of the most successful movies in history, earning more than $600 million worldwide. It received five Academy Award nominations, including a Best Actor nod for Johnny Depp.

Above: Actor Johnny Depp.

Right (left to right): Geoffrey Rush, Johnny Depp, Orlando Bloom, producer Jerry Bruckheimer, Keira Knightley, Jack Davenport.

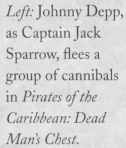

Left: Johnny Depp, as Captain Jack Sparrow, flees a group of cannibals in *Pirates of the Caribbean: Dead Man's Chest.*

Left (left to right): Jack Davenport as Commodore James Norrington, Orlando Bloom as Will Turner, and Johnny Depp as Captain Jack Sparrow.

Left: Johnny Depp in *Pirates of the Caribbean: Dead Man's Chest.*

The executives in charge of Walt Disney Pictures were so delighted that they quickly ordered two back-to-back sequels. The first, *Pirates of the Caribbean: Dead Man's Chest*, was released in the summer of 2006. The film performed even better than its predecessor, even though many critics didn't think it was as good as the original. Still, most fans were won over. By the end of 2006, it had made more than $1 billion worldwide, making it one of the most successful films ever.

The pirate adventure continues with 2007's *Pirates of the Caribbean: At World's End*, which finds the major characters reunited in a perilous journey at the edge of the world. Filming took place in locations in the Caribbean, Niagara Falls, Nevada's Bonneville Salt Flats, and off the coast of California.

The *Pirates of the Caribbean* trilogy reinvented and reinvigorated the pirate genre. Director Gore Verbinski doesn't see the need for a fourth film in the series. According to him, there's nothing much left to say when it comes to pirates. But as history has shown, the public's appetite for a good pirate story is never satisfied. There will undoubtedly be future pirate films. Shiver me timbers!

Facing page: Lobby poster for *Pirates of the Caribbean: Dead Man's Chest. Below (left to right):* Geoffrey Rush, Keira Knightley, and Johnny Depp in a scene from *Pirates of the Caribbean: At World's End.*

Computer Games

When gaming on personal computers became popular in the late 1980s and early 1990s, some software designers turned to pirates for inspiration. One of the first successful computer pirate games was LucasArts' *The Secret of Monkey Island*. This single-player, point-and-click adventure game was released in 1990. Beloved by gamers even today, it was known for its wacky humor, as well as its puzzles and delightful surprises. It also featured beautifully rendered screen art for its time.

Advanced computer graphics and challenging puzzles, however, are not the reasons why *The Secret of Monkey Island* became so popular. People loved the story, and the humor in the way it is told. Players take on the role of Guybrush Threepwood, a young man who wants to become a pirate. He is given three tasks to complete: find buried treasure, win a match of insult sword fighting, and steal a statue from the governor's mansion. Along the way, Guybrush falls in love with the governor, beautiful Elaine Marley. Unfortunately, the evil ghost pirate LeChuck has also fallen in love with Elaine. He kidnaps her and whisks her away to Monkey Island. Guybrush gathers a ragtag crew and sets sail to rescue his true love.

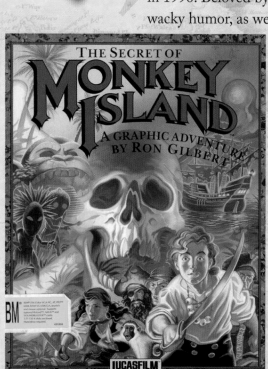

Above: The box cover to *The Secret of Monkey Island.*

Above: A screen shot from *Sid Meier's Pirates!*

The Secret of Monkey Island was developed by project leader Ron Gilbert, with help by Tim Schafer and Dave Grossman. It was the first video game to use character scaling; animated characters actually shrank or got bigger depending on where they were positioned on the screen. It sounds primitive by today's standards, but it was an innovative use of technology back in 1990. In keeping with the game's humor, the back of the game box advertised "eye-gouging 3D graphics," as well as "ear-piercing reggae music."

The game was so successful that it spawned three sequels: *Monkey Island 2: LeChuck's Revenge, The Curse of Monkey Island,* and *Escape from Monkey Island.* An upcoming fifth Monkey Island game is rumored, but LucasArts executives deny the game is in development for now.

Another very popular swashbuckling computer game is *Sid Meier's Pirates!* Developed by gaming legend Sid Meier and released by Firaxis Games in 2004, *Pirates!* is an action-adventure strategy game. Players take on the role of a 17th-century buccaneer, amassing fame and fortune by battling other sea captains and plundering hidden treasure. It is a richly detailed, open-ended game, similar in play to *The Sims.* Players move inside a massive game environment simulating the Caribbean, and interact with a huge cast of characters. There are many paths to winning the game, plus dozens of puzzles and mysteries to solve and secret islands to explore.

Originally published in 1987 as a popular PC computer game, *Sid Meier's Pirates!* has been updated to include advanced 3D graphics, which was impossible with the original 1980s computer technology. It is now available on Microsoft Windows and Xbox platforms.

Above: One of dozens of ships beautifully rendered in Flying Lab Software's massively multiplayer online game *Pirates of the Burning Sea.*

Flying Lab Software's *Pirates of the Burning Sea* is a massively multiplayer online (MMO) game for Windows-based personal computers. The game takes place in the Caribbean in 1720, during the Golden Age of Piracy. MMO games have potentially thousands of players all interacting in a virtual world, which never shuts down, even when players go offline.

In *Pirates of the Burning Sea*, players leave the real world behind and enter a 3D virtual world, becoming pirates, privateers, naval officers, or merchants. Every player is the captain of his or her own ship. Characters interact with the game world, or with other characters.

Players start the game aligned with one of four major powers: England, France, Spain, or Pirate. Action takes place in more than 100 ports throughout the entire Caribbean, including Jamaica, Dominica, Cuba, and islands in the Bahamas.

More than 1,000 missions keep players busy strengthening their characters, vanquishing enemies, or simply exploring hidden islands in fast sloops, looking for treasure or fame. Players earn ships, skills, and gear to become the most famous pirates on the high seas. You can challenge other characters to sword duels. Fighting also takes place in ship-to-ship battles. Players can even gang up, attacking enemy ships with their own group of friends.

Sophisticated naval combat happens in real-time. When you unleash a broadside of cannons at another man-of-war, you then have to decide whether to cut back to guard your damaged hull, or drop your sails and hope the enemy sails forward so you can fire again at his vulnerable stern. When the time is right, send a boarding party with grappling hooks to capture the enemy ship, or keep shooting and send your foe to Davy Jones' locker—the choice is yours. There are dozens of historically accurate ships to sail, and characters can even design their own flags.

Although ship-to-ship combat and swashbuckling adventures play a large part in *Pirates of the Burning Sea*, you can also choose to become a commercial trader, outsmarting pirates and getting rich inside a player-driven virtual economy. You can also create secret alliances with smugglers, or force ports to change sides. The game gives players the creative freedom to choose their own goals. Ultimately, it comes down to having fun. In an interview with *Massive Online Gamer* magazine, game producer John Scott Tynes said, "Everyone loves pirates. An exciting, swashbuckling, romantic adventure in the tradition of the classic pirate stories and movies is our primary goal."

Above: Two characters compete in a duel in this screenshot from *Pirates of the Burning Sea.* *Below:* A character witnesses a battle between ships.

27

Pirate Arrrt

Pirates have inspired some of the most creative artists in the world. The popular vision of a buccaneer's life is filled with romance and adventure, just the thing to fire the imagination of an artist. Howard Pyle (1853-1911) was an American illustrator who created many drawings for young people. He is most famous for his Robin Hood and King Arthur illustrations, but he also enjoyed painting pirates. *Howard Pyle's Book of Pirates,* which he wrote and illustrated, is a classic. Much of our concept of pirates comes from Pyle. His work was simple, but it had a sharp attention to detail and realism. Pyle was a student of history, which showed in his work. His pirate paintings are both thrilling and very believable.

Top right: Which Shall be Captain, by Howard Pyle. *Below:* An illustration from *Treasure Island,* by N.C. Wyeth.

American painter Newell Convers (N. C.) Wyeth (1882-1945) was a student of Howard Pyle. Wyeth learned to incorporate drama into his work. He also understood the importance of having a personal knowledge of his subjects, which gave his work a deep realism. His illustrations appeared on the covers of magazines such as *Harpers* and *The Saturday Evening Post.* Wyeth contributed several paintings to a 1911 edition of Robert Louis Stevenson's *Treasure Island,* which remains a pirate classic to this day.

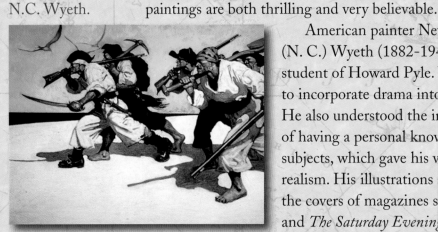

Artist Don Maitz has been an influential painter of pirates for more than 20 years. His work reflects what he calls "fantastic realism." He attended the Paier School of Art in Connecticut in the early 1970s, graduating at the top of his class. He eventually relocated to southern Florida, where he paints from his home-based art studio.

Maitz creates pirate illustrations featuring an exacting attention to historical detail combined with a lighthearted sense of humor. His vibrant colors and realistic perspectives make it seem as if his subjects are ready to walk right out of the canvas. He created the Captain Morgan spiced rum character. His work has been featured in *National Geographic* magazine, as well as exhibits in several museums around the country.

Above: Blackbeard's Revenge by Don Maitz.

Rowland Elzea, former chief curator of the Delaware Art Museum, said of the artist, "I appreciate the respect Don Maitz's work shows for that of the great imaginative illustrators of the past—Pyle, N. C. Wyeth, Dean Cornwall, to mention just a few—and how he has combined this great tradition with much of himself and the imagery of his time."

Left: Don the Pirate, a piratical self-portrait by artist Don Maitz.

Glossary

Bahamas
A group of islands in the western Atlantic Ocean, southeast of Florida and north of Cuba. Held as a British colony in the 18th and 19th centuries.

Booty
A pirate word meaning treasure, or plunder.

Broadside
When a warship simultaneously fires all its cannons on one side.

Buccaneers
Men who raided and captured ships, especially off the Spanish coasts of the Americas during the 17th and 18th centuries.

Caribbean
The islands and area of the Caribbean Sea, roughly the area between Florida and South and Central America.

Cutlass
A short, curved sword having a single sharp edge, often used by sailors.

Golden Age of Piracy
Roughly the years 1660 to 1740, the era when piracy was at its peak, especially along the coast of colonial America and in the Caribbean. Many former privateers, put out of work as peace spread across Europe, turned to piracy. The lack of a strong, central colonial government led to poor protection of ships at sea, at a time when many vessels carried valuables across the Atlantic Ocean.

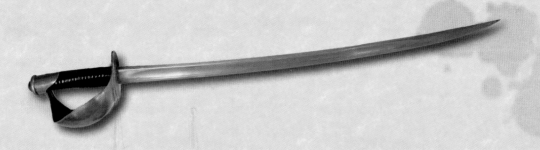

Grappling Hook

A hook with multiple prongs attached to a rope, designed to be thrown some distance to take hold of a target. They were used in naval warfare to ensnare the rigging or hull of an enemy ship so it could be drawn in and boarded.

Man-of-War

A large sailing warship armed with many cannons. These ships were used on the front line of battle.

Pirates

Rugged outlaw seamen who capture and raid ships at sea to seize their cargo and other valuables.

Privateer

A ship, or its captain and crew, operating under a letter of marque. A country issued letters of marque to permit the raiding of ships from specified countries that it had engaged in war. The captain and crew were paid out of any booty they took from the ships they attacked.

Above: Infamous Jolly John by Don Maitz.

Sloop

A fast single-masted sailing vessel with fore-and-aft rigging. Outfitted for war, it had a single gun deck, and usually carried up to 14 cannons. Most pirates preferred sloops because the ships were fast, could sail in shallow water, and were very maneuverable.

Index